YOUR PASSPORT TO

GUATEMALA

by Nancy Dickmann

raintree

a Capstone company — publishers for children

Raintree is an imprint of Capstone Global Library Limited, a company incorporated in England and Wales having its registered office at 264 Banbury Road, Oxford, OX2 7DY – Registered company number: 6695582

www.raintree.co.uk
myorders@raintree.co.uk

Edited by Clare Lewis
Designed by Juliette Peters
Original illustrations © Capstone Global Library Limited 2022
Picture research by Tracy Cummins
Production by Laura Manthe
Originated by Capstone Global Library Ltd
Printed and bound in India

978 1 3982 1508 5 (hardback)
978 1 3982 1507 8 (paperback)

British Library Cataloguing in Publication Data
A full catalogue record for this book is available from the British Library.

Acknowledgements
We would like to thank the following for permission to reproduce photographs: Alamy: Scott B. Rosen, 23; Capstone: Eric Gohl, 5; Getty Images: Ann Ronan Pictures/Print Collector, 8, Ian MacNicol/FIFA, 28, Sharpshooters/VW Pics/Universal Images Group, 19, Tony Barson/FilmMagic, 11; iStockphoto: Lucy Brown - loca4motion, 25, Rainer Soegtrop, 27; Shutterstock: Diego Grandi, 21, fboudrias, 13, Laura G. Robe, 15, Milosz Maslanka, 17, Ondrej Prosicky, 7, Rob Crandall, 16, ROSITO, 14, salmon-negro, 20, SL-Photography, Cover, WitR, 9. Design elements: iStockphoto: Yevhenii Dubinko; Shutterstock: Flipser, Gil C, KASUE, MicroOne, pingebat

CONTENTS

Words in **bold** are in the glossary.

CHAPTER ONE

WELCOME TO GUATEMALA!

The rainforest is hot and humid. Brightly coloured birds fly through the trees. A crumbling **temple** rises above the treetops. This is the ancient site of Tikal in Guatemala. People called the Maya built it thousands of years ago. Today, people come from all over the world to visit it.

Guatemala is a small country in Central America. More than 17 million people live there. Many of them are Maya. They still speak Maya languages. Many other people are a mix of Maya and Spanish. Spanish soldiers arrived in the 1500s. They controlled Guatemala for many years. Their **descendants** still speak Spanish today.

MAP OF GUATEMALA

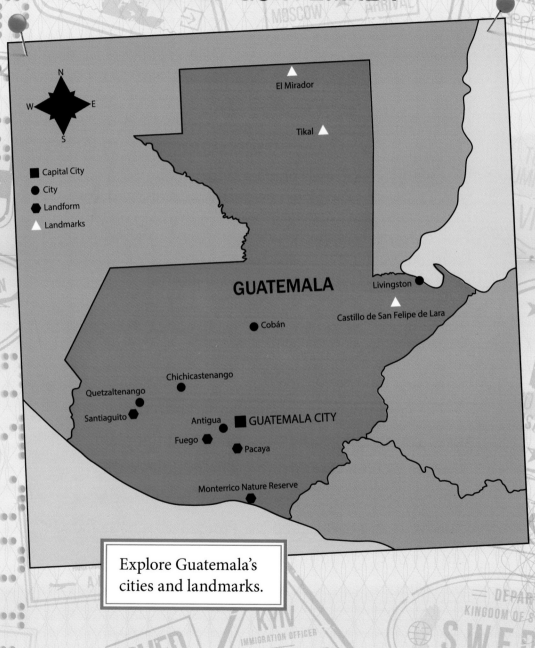

- N
- W E
- S

- ■ Capital City
- ● City
- ⬡ Landform
- ▲ Landmarks

El Mirador ▲

Tikal ▲

GUATEMALA

Livingston ●

Castillo de San Felipe de Lara ▲

Cobán ●

Chichicastenango ●

Quetzaltenango ●

Santiaguito ⬡

Antigua ⬡ ■ GUATEMALA CITY

Fuego ⬡

Pacaya ⬡

Monterrico Nature Reserve ⬡

Explore Guatemala's
cities and landmarks.

FACT FILE

OFFICIAL NAME: ....REPUBLIC OF GUATEMALA
POPULATION: 17,889,773
LAND AREA: ....107,159 SQ KM (41,374 SQ. MI.)
CAPITAL: ....GUATEMALA CITY
MONEY: ....QUETZAL
GOVERNMENT: ..............................PRESIDENTIAL REPUBLIC
LANGUAGE: ....SPANISH AND MANY MAYA LANGUAGES
GEOGRAPHY: Guatemala borders Mexico to the north and west. El Salvador and Honduras are to the south, and Belize is to the northeast. Guatemala has a long coastline on the Pacific Ocean and a shorter one on the Caribbean Sea.
NATURAL RESOURCES: Guatemala has metals, rubber and oil. It also grows sugar cane, bananas and coffee.

THREE PARTS

The land in Guatemala is divided into three main parts. Along the Pacific coast, there is a flat plain. The land is good for farming. The middle of the country has mountains and valleys. In the north, there is a large area called the Petén. It is mostly flat and covered in rainforests. Many Maya ruins are found here.

Ancient Maya rulers used the quetzal's feathers to make headdresses.

NATIONAL BIRD

A bird called the quetzal lives in the rainforest. It has bright blue, green and red feathers. Males have tail feathers up to 1 metre (3 feet) long! This bird is a symbol of Guatemala. The country's currency is named after it.

CHAPTER TWO

HISTORY OF GUATEMALA

Civilization in Guatemala began about 4,000 years ago. People started to farm the land and set up towns. They made pottery and created art. By about 800 BC, there were many villages. They traded with each other and began to build larger buildings.

By about AD 200, the Maya had built grand cities. They had temples, palaces and large open squares. The Maya had **irrigation** systems for watering their crops. They had a complex system of writing. They wrote stories and recorded events on paper made from tree bark and on huge stone tablets.

Maya writing used symbols called glyphs.

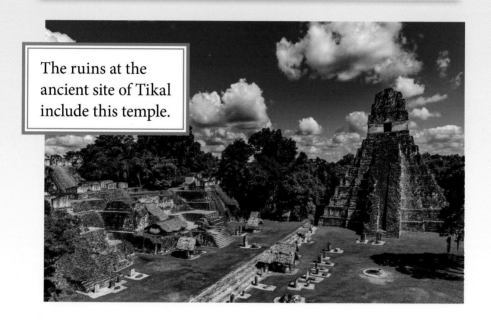

The ruins at the ancient site of Tikal include this temple.

THE SPANISH ARRIVE

The first Spanish soldiers arrived in Guatemala in 1524. They had guns and horses, which the Maya didn't. The Spanish soon took over. Many of the Maya were killed. Others died from disease. Many of them were forced to work for the Spanish.

TIMELINE OF GUATEMALAN HISTORY

ABOUT 2000 BC: People start to farm and build settlements in Guatemala.

ABOUT AD 250: The Maya begin to organize into city-states, each with its own king.

ABOUT AD 900: Maya sites start to be abandoned.

1524: Spanish soldiers under the command of Pedro de Alvarado arrive in Guatemala.

1821: A group of *criollos* declare Guatemala to be independent.

1847: Guatemala becomes a republic.

1941: Guatemala enters World War II on the side of the Allies.

1960: A civil war begins between the government and the poor and indigenous populations.

1992: Rigoberta Menchú wins the Nobel Peace Prize for her fight for the rights of indigenous people in Guatemala.

1996: A ceasefire ends the civil war. Many Maya communities are left devastated.

INDEPENDENCE

The Spanish controlled Guatemala for nearly 300 years. But in the early 1800s, a group called *criollos* became more powerful. These people were descended from the Spanish. But they had been born in Guatemala. Many of them owned large areas of land. They wanted to rule themselves. They and other groups began to fight for their independence.

In 1821, Guatemala became **independent** from Spain. But the country's Maya were still not truly free. The criollos ruled over them.

CIVIL WAR

In the years after independence, Guatemala had many different rulers. In 1960, a terrible **civil war** began. Many poor people banded together to fight the government. They included many of the country's **indigenous** people. The war finally ended in 1996.

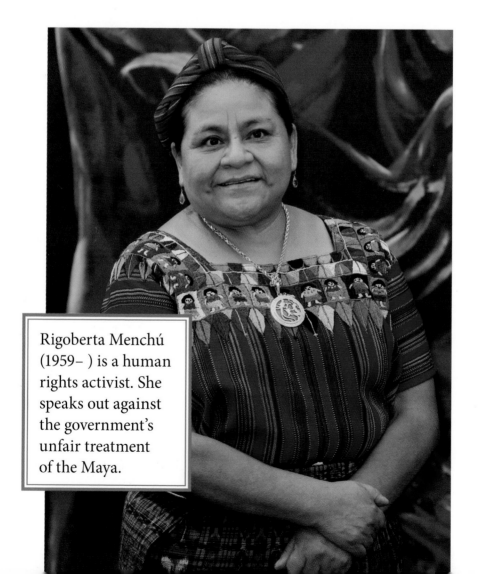

Rigoberta Menchú (1959–) is a human rights activist. She speaks out against the government's unfair treatment of the Maya.

CHAPTER THREE

EXPLORE GUATEMALA

Tourists come to Guatemala for its beautiful scenery. The country has mountains and lakes. There are also beautiful beaches. The dense rainforests are filled with wildlife. Tourists also come to see Maya culture and sites. They visit the country's modern cities too.

VOLCANOES

Guatemala has more than twenty **volcanoes**. They stretch out in a line that runs from the Mexican border to the border with El Salvador. Many of the volcanoes are dormant. This means they haven't erupted for a long time. Others are extinct. They will probably never erupt. But three of them are still active! They are called Fuego, Santiaguito and Pacaya.

FACT
|||||||||||||

The Fuego volcano had a
very large eruption in 2018.

BEACHES

Guatemala's beaches are among its secret treasures. Many of them are rarely crowded. Surfers enjoy the pounding waves. People take boats out to fish or to spot whales. The beach at Monterrico is part of a nature reserve. Sea turtles come here each year to lay eggs.

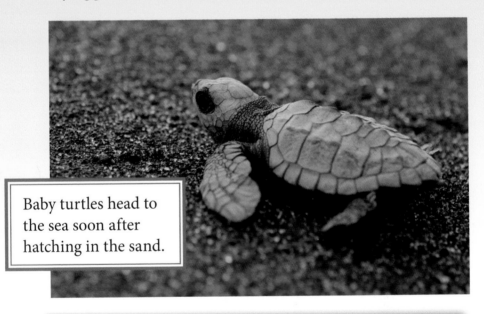

Baby turtles head to the sea soon after hatching in the sand.

FACT

The sand on some of Guatemala's beaches is black. It is made from cooled lava. Over many years, the pounding waves have turned it into sand.

BEAUTIFUL CITIES

Guatemala City is the country's largest city. It is a busy city with modern buildings. Most of the older buildings were destroyed in earthquakes in 1917 and 1918. Tourists often visit Antigua instead. This city was founded by the Spanish in 1543. There are cobbled streets and old churches.

Quetzaltenango is in the western part of the country. It is the largest city in the Maya region. Tourists also visit the smaller town of Chichicastenango. It has a huge open-air market. People sell fabric, pottery and other Maya crafts.

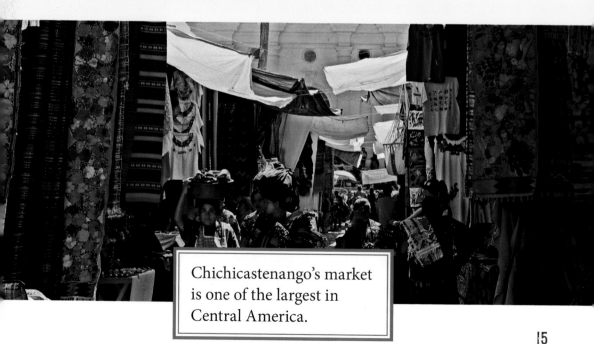

Chichicastenango's market is one of the largest in Central America.

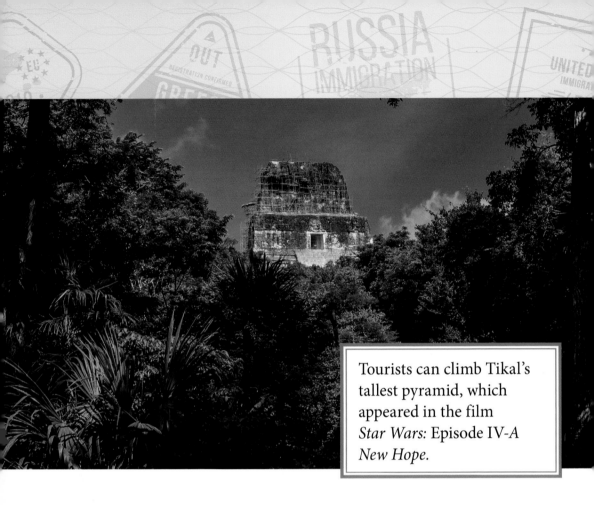

Tourists can climb Tikal's tallest pyramid, which appeared in the film *Star Wars:* Episode IV-*A New Hope.*

ANCIENT SITES

Guatemala's Maya heritage attracts many tourists. They visit villages where Maya people still live today. They also visit the ancient sites built by these people's **ancestors**. Tikal is the most famous site. It has five steep pyramids built of stone. They served as temples. One of them is 65 metres (212 feet) tall. Some visitors climb to the top. They can see other temples poking through the trees.

Tikal has thousands of other buildings. **Archaeologists** have discovered tombs and palaces. There are also courts where the Maya played a ball game. Teams tried to get a rubber ball through a hoop.

El Mirador is another stunning Maya site. It is even bigger than Tikal. But it is deep in the rainforest. Few tourists make it this far.

CASTILLO DE SAN FELIPE DE LARA

In about 1652, the Spanish built a fort along the Dulce River. It guarded the entrance to Lake Izabal. It was designed to keep pirates from looting the port along the lake's coast. However, pirates did capture the fort at least once. In later years, it was used as a prison.

CHAPTER FOUR

DAILY LIFE

About half of Guatemalans live in rural areas. Many of them live in the north of the country. They live in small villages and farm the land. Most of the people in the north are Maya. They often still wear traditional clothes. They speak more than twenty different Maya languages. Their religion is a mix of Christian and Maya beliefs.

Life in the countryside is not always easy. There are few doctors. Children may have to travel a long way to school. Some of them work on farms instead of going to school. The average age for leaving school is 11.

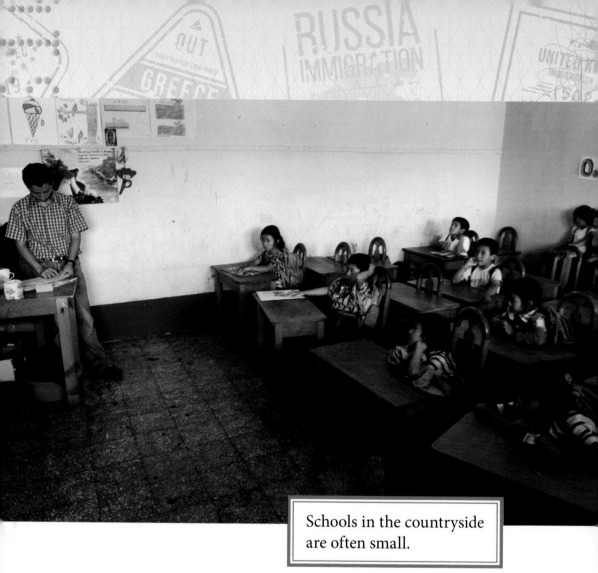

Schools in the countryside are often small.

THE GARIFUNA

A group called the Garifuna live in Guatemala. Their ancestors were enslaved people from Africa. The enslaved people were taken from Africa to work in the Caribbean. They rebelled to try to free themselves and were sent away from the Caribbean. Many ended up settling in Guatemala.

FARMING

There are many farms in Guatemala. Volcanic **lava** has made the soil rich. It is very good for growing crops. People grow corn, beans and other vegetables to eat. Farmers also grow crops to sell to other countries. They include coffee, sugar, bananas and spices.

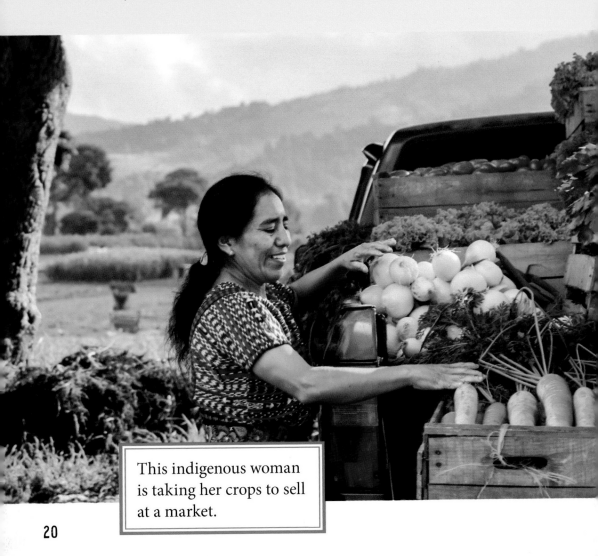

This indigenous woman is taking her crops to sell at a market.

CITY LIFE

About 3 million people live in Guatemala City. Many others live in smaller cities and towns. City life is different from that in the countryside. There are shops, restaurants and parks. There are traffic jams too!

Guatemalans are known for being friendly and laid-back. Family life is very important. Several generations of the same family will often live together. Many Guatemalans have moved to the United States to work. They send money to support their families back home.

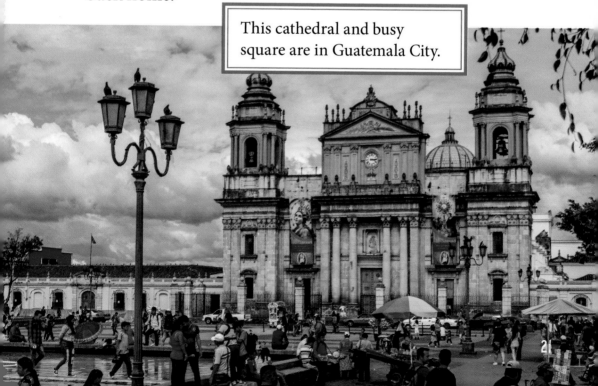

This cathedral and busy square are in Guatemala City.

FOOD AND DRINK

Guatemalans enjoy sharing meals with family and friends. The food is a mix of Maya and Spanish traditions. There are African and Caribbean influences too. Many dishes are based on tortillas, corn, pork, chicken and cheese. There are also tropical fruits such as mangoes and avocados.

POPULAR DISHES

There are two classic dishes that are eaten across the country. One is chicken *pepián*. It is a spicy stew of chicken, fruit and vegetables. It is served with rice and tortillas. The other meal is *kak'ik*. This is a turkey soup with chillis. The recipe goes back to Maya times.

For a quick snack, many people eat empanadas. These crispy pastries are often filled with potato and spinach. They are often served with guacamole.

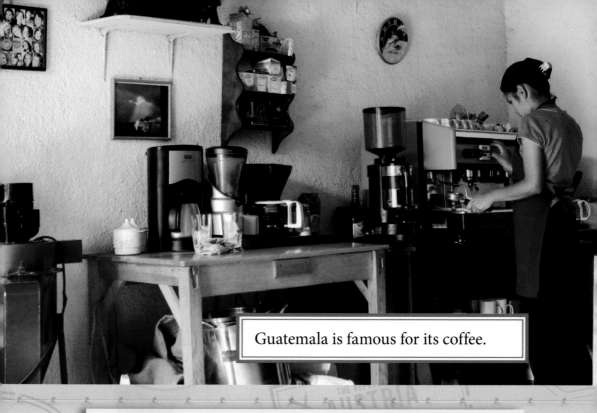

Guatemala is famous for its coffee.

HOT CHOCOLATE

Guatemala is sometimes called "the birthplace of chocolate". To the Maya, it was the food of the gods. It was traditionally served as a drink and it still is today.

Ingredients:
- hot chocolate bars
- milk
- cinnamon stick (or ground cinnamon)

Instructions:

1. For each serving, you will need 1–2 squares of chocolate and 1 cup of milk. One cinnamon stick is enough for two servings.
2. Put the chocolate, milk and cinnamon into a saucepan.
3. Ask an adult to help you heat it gently, stirring occasionally, until the chocolate is dissolved.
4. Remove the cinnamon stick and whisk the chocolate to make it frothy.
5. Serve while still hot.

CHAPTER FIVE

HOLIDAYS AND CELEBRATIONS

Most people in Guatemala are Christian. This means that Christian festivals are very important. The week before Easter is Holy Week. People march through the streets carrying religious statues. In Antigua, people make colourful patterns on the streets. These pictures are called *alfombras*. They are made from coloured sawdust.

Christmas celebrations start on 7 December. People set fire to little piñatas that represent the devil. In the nine days before Christmas, they celebrate *Las Posadas*. Every night there is a procession. People carry lanterns and statues of Joseph and Mary.

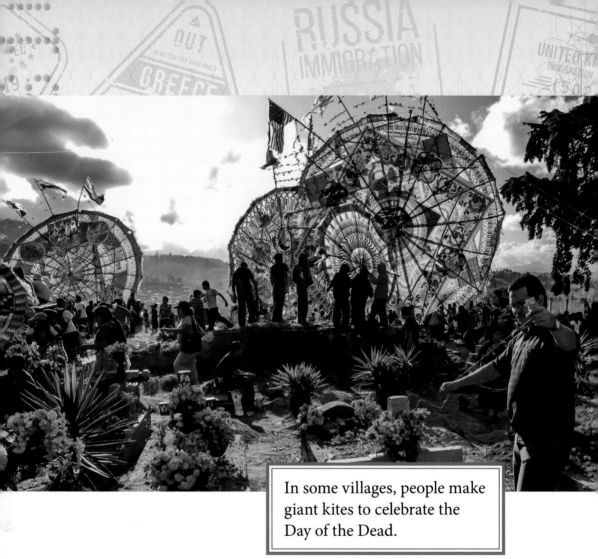

In some villages, people make giant kites to celebrate the Day of the Dead.

DAY OF THE DEAD

On 1 and 2 November, Guatemalans remember loved ones who have died. It is called the Day of the Dead. People visit graves and say prayers. There is music and dancing. It is a sad time, but a happy one too.

INDEPENDENCE DAY

The whole country celebrates on 15 September. This is the day that Guatemala won its independence from Spain. People fly the Guatemalan blue and white flag and dress in those colours too. There are fireworks and parades with marching bands. Runners carry torches from village to village.

FOLK FESTIVALS

The city of Cobán hosts a folklore festival every summer. There are parades and exhibits of traditional art. There is Maya music and dancing. Girls wear Maya clothes to compete in a beauty pageant. The winner is crowned "Maya princess".

The famous *Palo Volador* is performed at several festivals. Its name means *flying pole*. Two dancers climb to the top of a tall pole. Then they jump off. Held by ropes, they hold poses and spin gradually to the ground. This ritual has been performed since ancient Maya times.

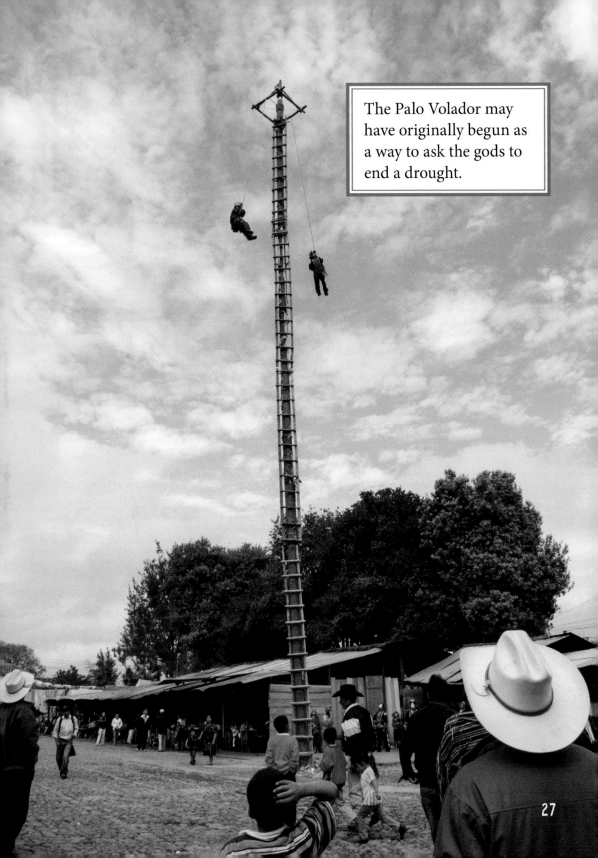

The Palo Volador may have originally begun as a way to ask the gods to end a drought.

CHAPTER SIX

SPORT AND RECREATION

Football is the most popular sport in Guatemala. People support the Guatemalan national team. The team hopes to qualify for a World Cup tournament soon. They have won other competitions.

Futsal is also popular in Guatemala. This is a type of football played on a hard court, usually indoors. There are five players on each team. Many people play for fun. The national team is also very successful.

Many of today's top professional footballers got their start playing futsal.

OTHER SPORTS

Many people in Guatemala play baseball. Kayaking is also popular. There are volcanoes to climb and caves to explore. There is something for everyone in Guatemala!

CINCOS

Cincos is a simple marble game played by children in Guatemala. You need two or more players, an area of ground to play on, and some marbles shared equally.

1. Draw a triangle on the ground. Each player puts one of their marbles inside.
2. Players take turns throwing or flicking a marble into the triangle, trying to knock one of the other players' marbles out.
3. If you knock someone's marble out, you get to keep it. If the marble that you used to knock it out stays inside the triangle, you get another turn.
4. If you don't hit anyone's marble, the marble that you threw stays inside the triangle. You can pick it up on your next turn if no one has knocked it out by then.
5. The game ends when all the marbles are knocked out of the triangle. The player with the most marbles wins.

GLOSSARY

ancestor
person from whom
someone is descended,
many generations ago

archaeologist
person who studies human
history by digging historic
sites and finding things

civil war
war fought between
different groups within
a country, rather than
between different countries

descendant
originally coming
from a certain group,
generations ago

independent
not ruled over by
anyone else

indigenous
native to a place

irrigation
way of supplying water to
land to help crops grow

lava
hot, molten rock that
comes out of a volcano
when it erupts

temple
sacred building where
religious rituals take place

volcano
mountain with a crater at
the top, through which
lava, gas and ash can erupt

FIND OUT MORE

BOOKS

Daily Life in the Maya Civilization (Daily Life in Ancient Civilizations), Nick Hunter (Raintree, 2016)

The Mayans (History Hunters), Louise Spilsbury (Raintree, 2016)

Our World in Pictures: Countries, Cultures, People and Places: A Visual Encyclopedia of the World, DK (DK Children, 2020)

WEBSITES

www.bbc.co.uk/bitesize/topics/zq6svcw/articles/zndq7p3
What happened to the Mayas?

www.dkfindout.com/uk/earth/volcanoes
Find out more about volcanoes.

INDEX

OTHER BOOKS IN THIS SERIES